THE SINGLE PARENT SURVIVAL GUIDE

Copyright © 1987 by Michael Sack and Marion Keen
Published by Price Stern Sloan, Inc.
360 North La Cienega Boulevard, Los Angeles, California 90048

Printed in the United States of America. All rights reserved. No part of this publication may be reproduced, stored in a retrieval system or transmitted in any form or by any means, electronic, mechanical, photocopying, recording or otherwise, without the prior written permission of the publishers.

ISBN: 0-8431-2254-4

THE SINGLE PARENT SURVIVAL GUIDE

BY MICHAEL SACK AND MARION KEEN

PRICE STERN SLOAN, INC.
Los Angeles

For John and Stan

...YOU'RE PICKING THE KIDS UP AT 4:30?— BUT I HAVE A MEETING 'TIL 6:45! SURE, PICK UP MARY-FRANCIS AT SCHOOL—SHE'S GOT TO BE AT THE ORTHODONTIST AT 4:00—FILLMORE'S AT SCOTT'S HOUSE TODAY—TEACHERS' MEETING—PICK HIM UP THERE!...C'MON!!! THE BROWN HOUSE BEHIND THE 7-ELEVEN...REMEMBER, HAVE SOMETHING SOFT FOR DINNER—MARY-FRANCIS IS HAVING HER BANDS TIGHTENED..FILLMORE HAS HIS FIRST SOCCER GAME TOMORROW MORNING AT 10:00...THAT'S TOO BAD!—WELL, GO BY THE HOUSE AND PICK UP THEIR STUFF! BY-THE-WAY, I DIDN'T HAVE TIME TO GET THE LAUNDRY DONE...IT'S IN THAT SACK IN THE HALL....AND WHY NOT? YOU'VE GOT A WASHER AND DRYER TOO!!— OH, HOW MANY BOXES OF COOKIES WILL YOU TAKE?—WHAT DO YOU MEAN NONE!...BUT SHE CAN SELL SOME IN THE BUILDING?.......NO, I CAN'T SWITCH WEEKENDS ON THE 26TH—I'VE MADE PLANS O.K.!! -YOU CHANGE YOUR PLANS THEN!!........ I AM NOT!!............ YOU'RE BRINGING THEM BACK WHEN?
WEEKLY PLANNER

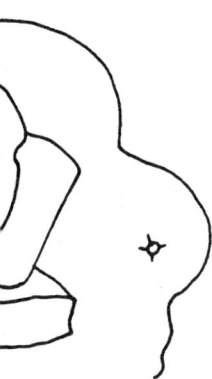

"IT'S A DIRECT LINE TO MY BABYSITTER."

THE SITTER

"WHAT MOUSSE?"

...WHAT D'YA MEAN: IT'S THE LUCK OF THE DRAW ?? WHEN KIDS ARE SICK, THEY NEED THEIR MOTHER!!!

...BET I CAN TRADE THIS FOR TWO CUPCAKES, A COUPLE DING-DONGS AND A TWINKIE!

WHO'LL TRADE A PEANUT BUTTER SANDWICH FOR A GOURMET LUNCH?
WHAT'S THAT SMELL?

THE SINGLE-PARENT'S MOST

FREQUENT DINNER COMPANIONS

...NEXT WEEKEND AT YOUR PLACE?
...I CAN'T........ JENNIFER AND MICHAEL WILL BE HOME... HOW ABOUT THE 26TH?

I CAN'T... IT'S MY WEEKEND TO HAVE JOSHUA, ZACHARY AND ISABELLE........ HOW ABOUT.......... ....?

ARE YOU KIDS ALL PACKED? DADDY'S PICKING YOU UP IN TEN MINUTES!
YOU'RE GOING TO BE SO LONESOME THIS WEEKEND-AREN'T YOU, MOMMY?

DON'T WORRY. WE'LL BE BACK! DADDY SAYS HE CAN ONLY TAKE US FOR TWO DAYS AT A TIME!

SHOPPING
SLEEP
DINNER DATE
MOVIE

YOU'RE GOING TO MISS US ALOT- AREN'T YOU, MOMMY?

"...BEEN AWHILE SINCE YOU'VE GONE DANCING, RIGHT?"

...SOMEWHERE, DEEP INSIDE IS A REAL PERSON WITH A REAL NAME — NOT MOM, NOT MOMMY, NOT JENNIFER AND MICHAEL'S MOTHER .... NO LUCK? .... O.K. IMAGINE YOU'RE WRITING A CHECK — WHAT NAME ARE YOU SIGNING?
MRS...??

SUPERMARKET
IS THIS WHERE YOU'RE GOING TO GET US A SURPRISE, DADDY?

SHE'S CUTE!
FRESH SPIN
HEY! SPINACH IS NO SUPRISE!

—I THINK HE'S GOING TO GET OUR SURPRISE NEXT!

NOT BAD.....
BEETS
OLD YUCKY BEETS!

HMmmm!
-HE WOULD'NT GIVE US RED-HOT CHILI-PEPPERS FOR A SURPRISE!
...... WOULD HE??

CAT FOOD
KITTY
-HEY FILLMORE!! WE'RE GETTIN' A CAT!!!
PLOP!
CAT CHOW
KAT
CAT

GRIDLOCK!! I'VE GOT MORE MONEY IN MY ACCOUNT THAN I THOUGHT!
....I COULD BUY A NEW DRESS FOR SUCCESS WARDROBE, OR..........

I COULD JOIN THAT NEW HEALTH CLUB AND SPA..
...OR, SPEND A WEEKEND AT AN OCEANSIDE RESORT, OR.......
RING
RING
RING
HELLO?...THIS IS THE SCHOOL NURSE — MARY-FRANCIS NEEDS GLASSES!
..... HELLO ..... HELLO ?????

LET'S PLAY HOUSE! YOU BE MY DATE AN' YOU'RE TAKING ME OUT FOR DINNER!
—I JUST LOVE YOUNGER MEN!

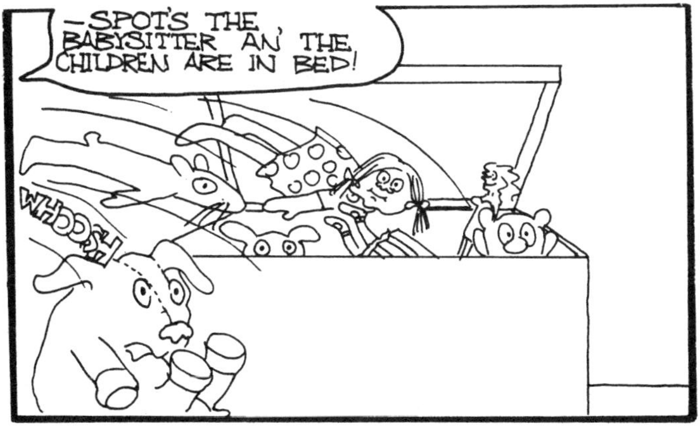
—SPOT'S THE BABYSITTER AN' THE CHILDREN ARE IN BED!
WHOOOSH

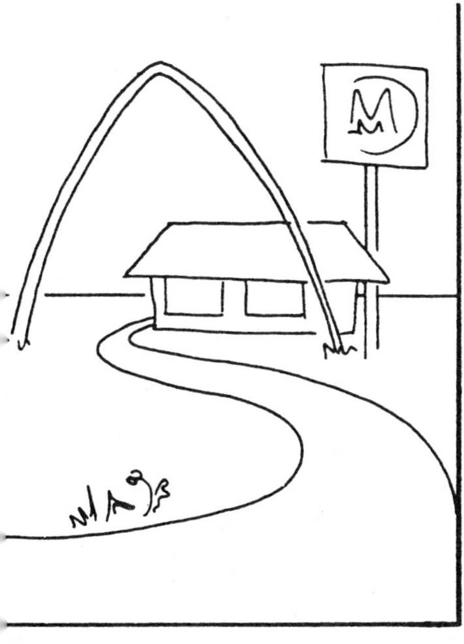

Mary Francis Fillmore Gridlock

DADDY SAYS WE'RE GOING TO CAMP OUT.... HIGH UP UNDER THE STARS!!

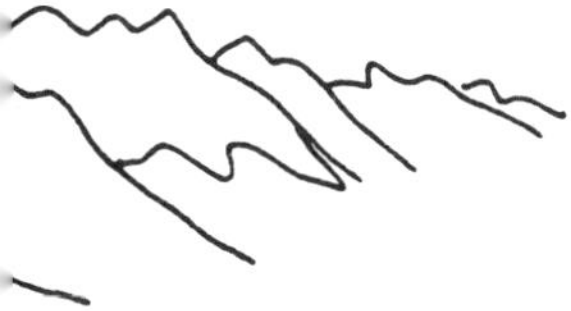

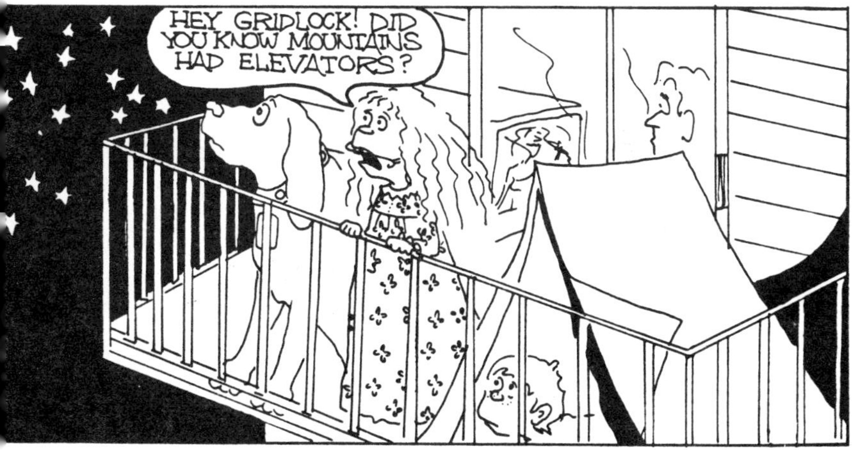
HEY GRIDLOCK! DID YOU KNOW MOUNTAINS HAD ELEVATORS?

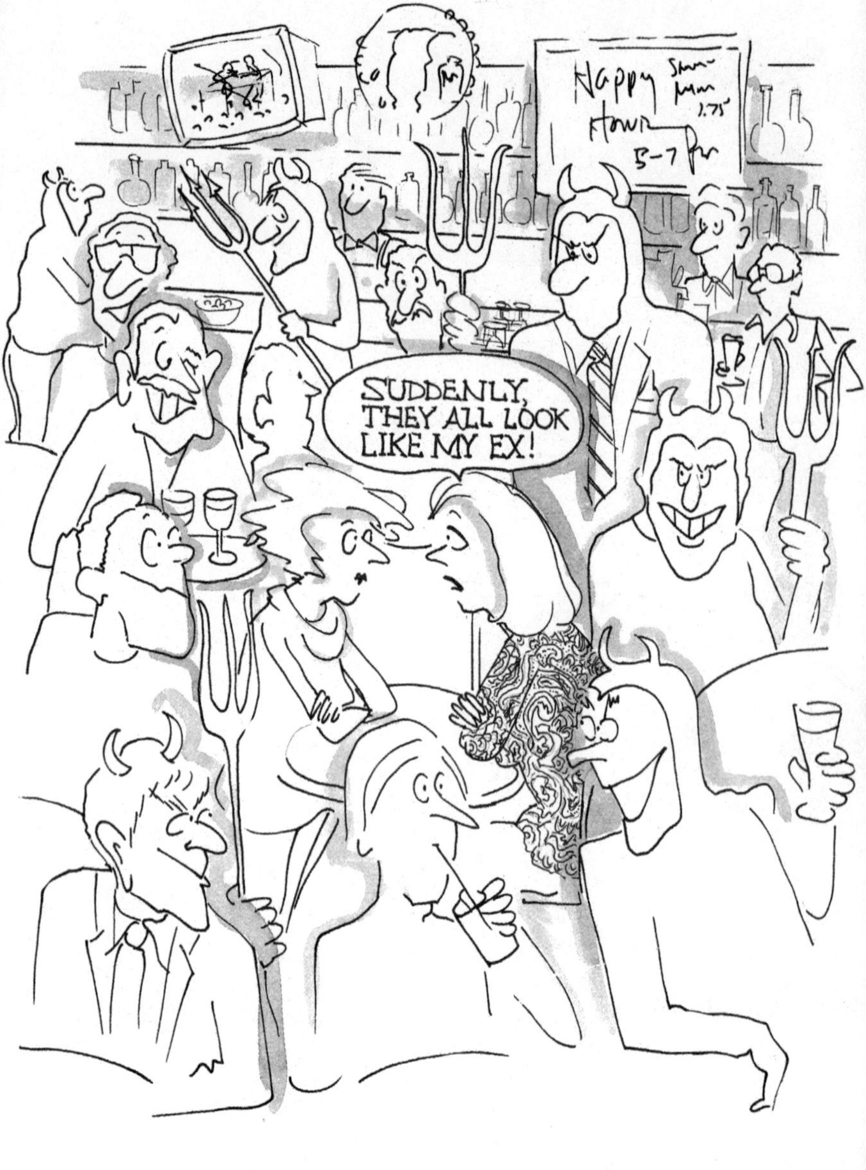
SUDDENLY, THEY ALL LOOK LIKE MY EX!

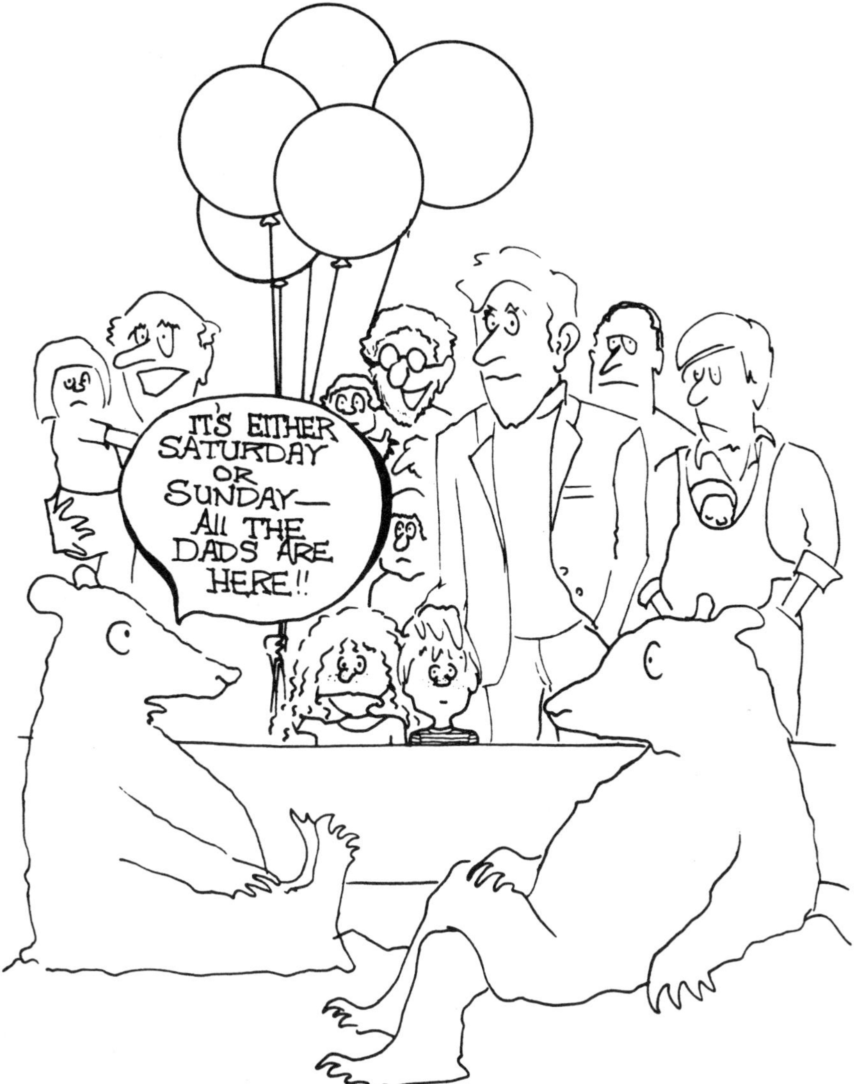
IT'S EITHER SATURDAY OR SUNDAY— ALL THE DADS ARE HERE!!

...BECAUSE HELIUM IS LIGHTER THAN AIR IT MAKES BALLOONS GO UP. SURE, IF YOU HAD ENOUGH OF THEM IT........

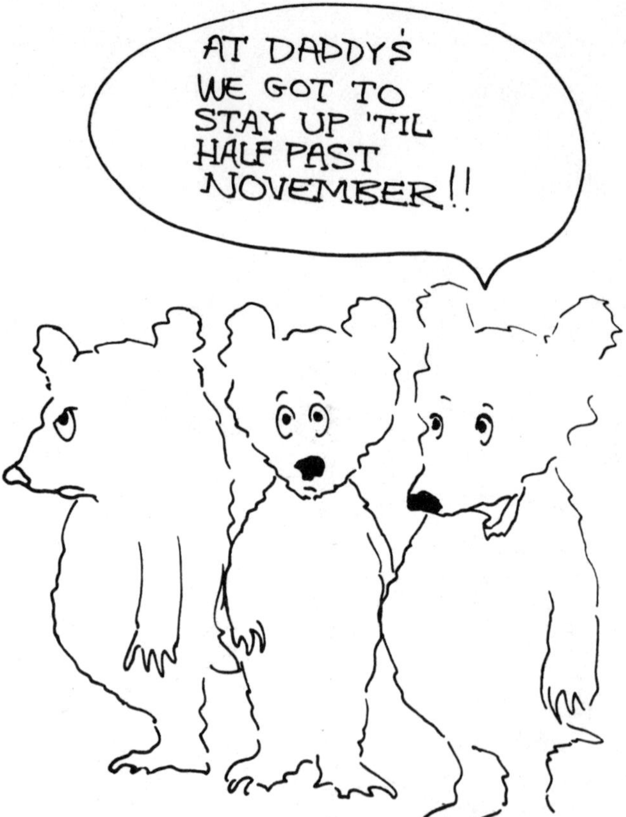
AT DADDY'S WE GOT TO STAY UP 'TIL HALF PAST NOVEMBER!!

—PUT DOWN THAT CORN COB— I WANT YOU IN THAT MUD AND I WANT YOU IN THERE NOW!
NO BUTS ABOUT IT!!

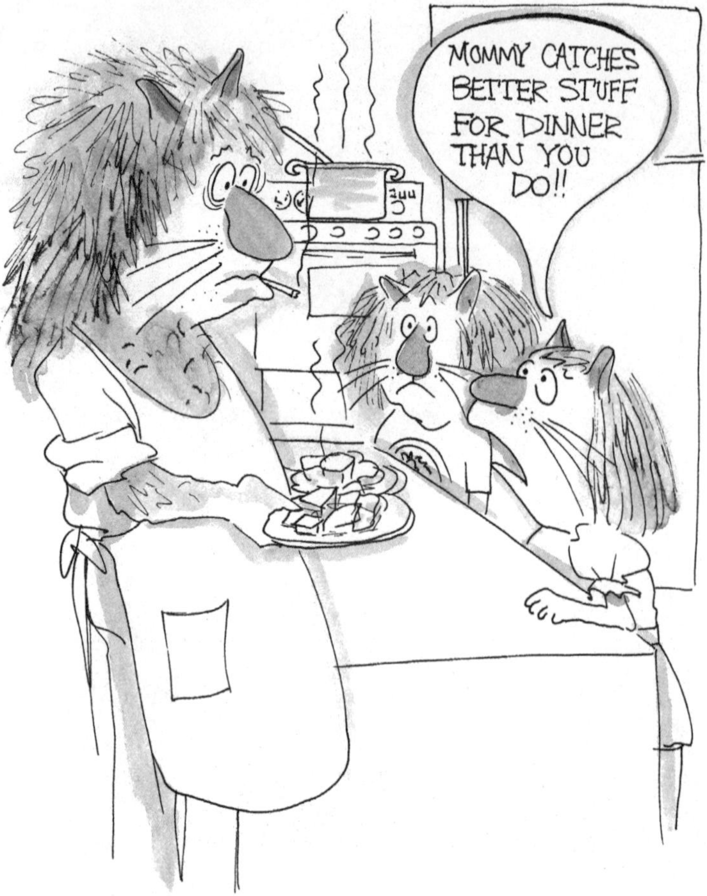
MOMMY CATCHES BETTER STUFF FOR DINNER THAN YOU DO!!

MARTIN WAS A WINTER PERSON — BUT IF I DON'T GET MY SLEEP, I'M A PERFECT WRECK IN THE SPRING!!

...YOU LISTEN TO ME BUSTER! I WANT THOSE TEETH FIXED AND YOU'RE GOING TO ASSUME SOME RESPONSIBILITY!!

AT FIRST IT WAS A DRINK EVERY COUPLE OF MONTHS– THEN IT WAS *EVERY* MONTH – BUT WHEN IT GOT TO BE EVERY *WEEK*.... I TOOK EMILY AND LEFT!

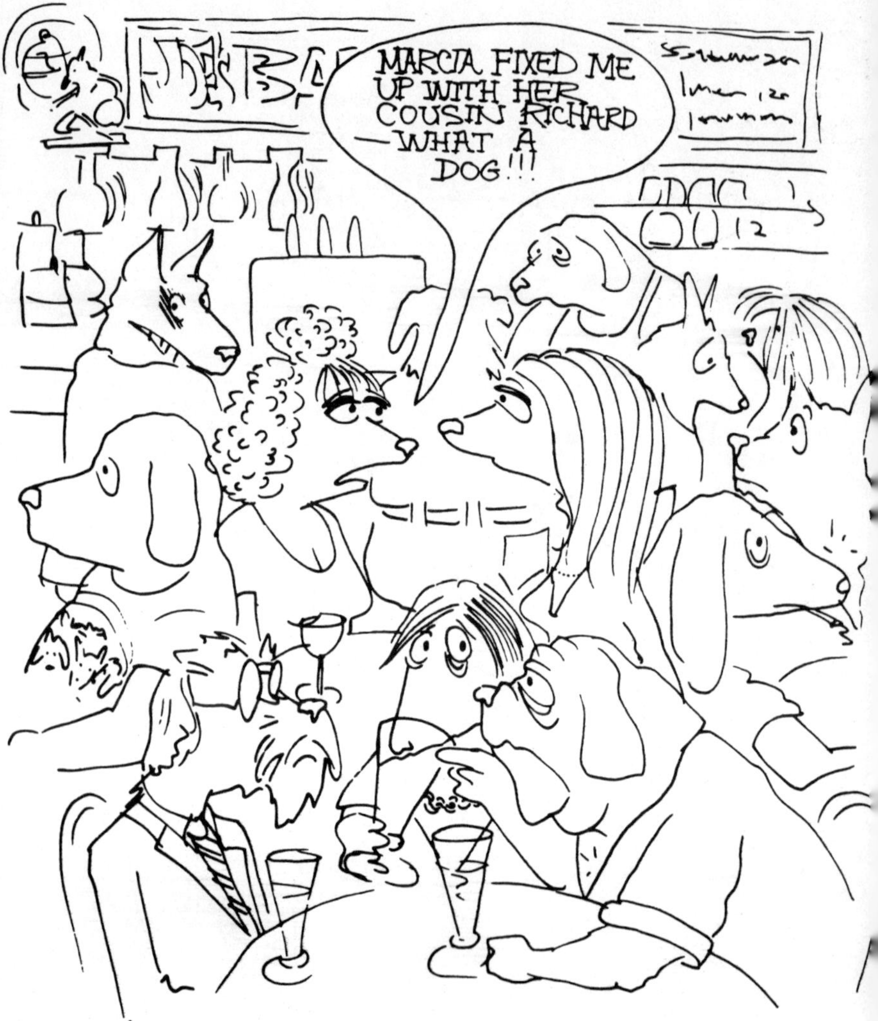
MARCIA FIXED ME UP WITH HER COUSIN RICHARD —WHAT A DOG!!!

"WHEN MY DAUGHTER ASKED MY IDEA OF HEAVEN, I SAID — THREE WEEKS AT THE GOLDEN DOOR!"

"I SEE DADDY'S GIVEN YOU

A FEW GIFTS AGAIN!"

TALL, RUGGED, MALE-PROFESSIONAL SEEKS MATURE, TRIM, INTELLIGENT FEMALE TO SHARE LOVE OF MUSIC, THEATRE, TENNIS, GOURMET COOKING. RESPOND BOX 215 FOR POSSIBLE LASTING RELATIONSHIP. WOW!
PERSONALS

OH BOY! SLIM, VIBRANT BLOND SEEKING BRIGHT, MOTIVATED MALE 35-45 FOR COMPANIONSHIP AND GOOD TIMES ON LONG-TERM BASIS. BOX 3771
PERSONALS

.....TONIGHT! I'M GOING TO MEET MY TALL, MATURE, RUGGED PROFESSIONAL— I JUST KNOW HE'LL BE MR RIGHT!

.....WE'RE MEETING TONIGHT AND I'VE GOT A FEELING THAT SHE'S THE ONE I'VE BEEN LOOKING FOR, EVER SINCE THE DIVORCE.

...O.K. BRING ON THE SLIM VIBRANT BLOND!
OH NO
IT'S MY EX!

HEY MOMMY, CAN I GET A TRAINING BRA?

WEEKEND WITH DAD
THERE'S SOMEONE I WANT YOU KIDS TO MEET—

...NOT UNTIL YOU'RE OLDER!

FILLMORE, MARY-FRANCIS, THIS IS BEVERLY!
MOMMY SAYS I'M NOT OLD ENOUGH FOR A TRAINING-BRA! —FOR-CRYIN'-OUT-LOUD, HOW OLD DO YA HAFTA BE TO GET ONE??

A SINGLE FATHER IS SIGHTED

AT THE "PARENTS-WITHOUT-PARTNERS" PICNIC.

FITNESS CLUB

TO MEET MEN YOU HAVE TO BE WHERE MEN ARE.
THINK OF PLACES YOU'D FIND LOTS OF MEN AND GO THERE!
?

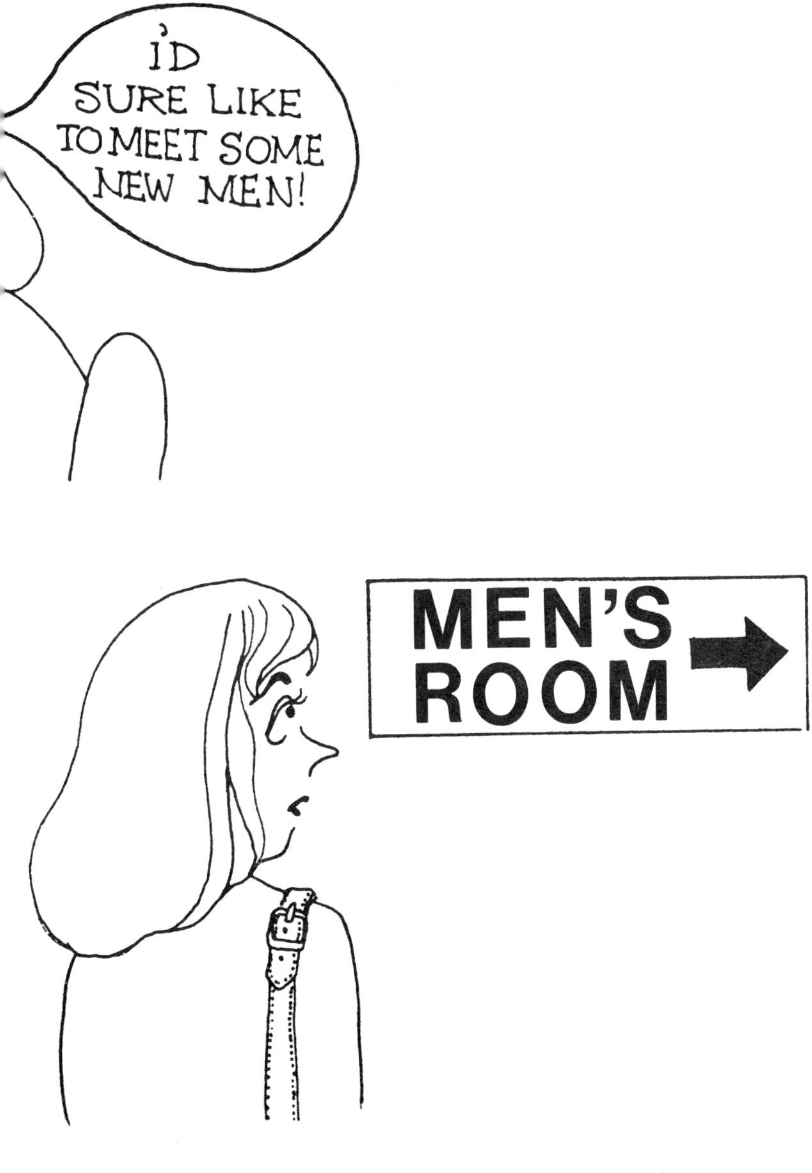
I'D SURE LIKE TO MEET SOME NEW MEN!
MEN'S ROOM

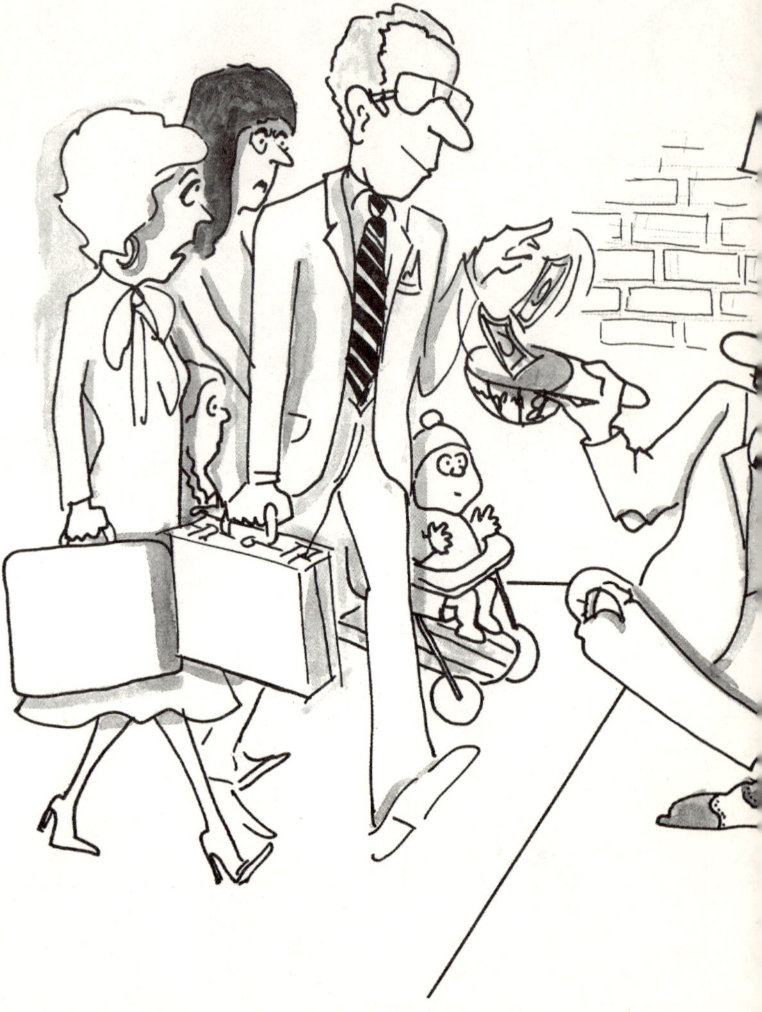

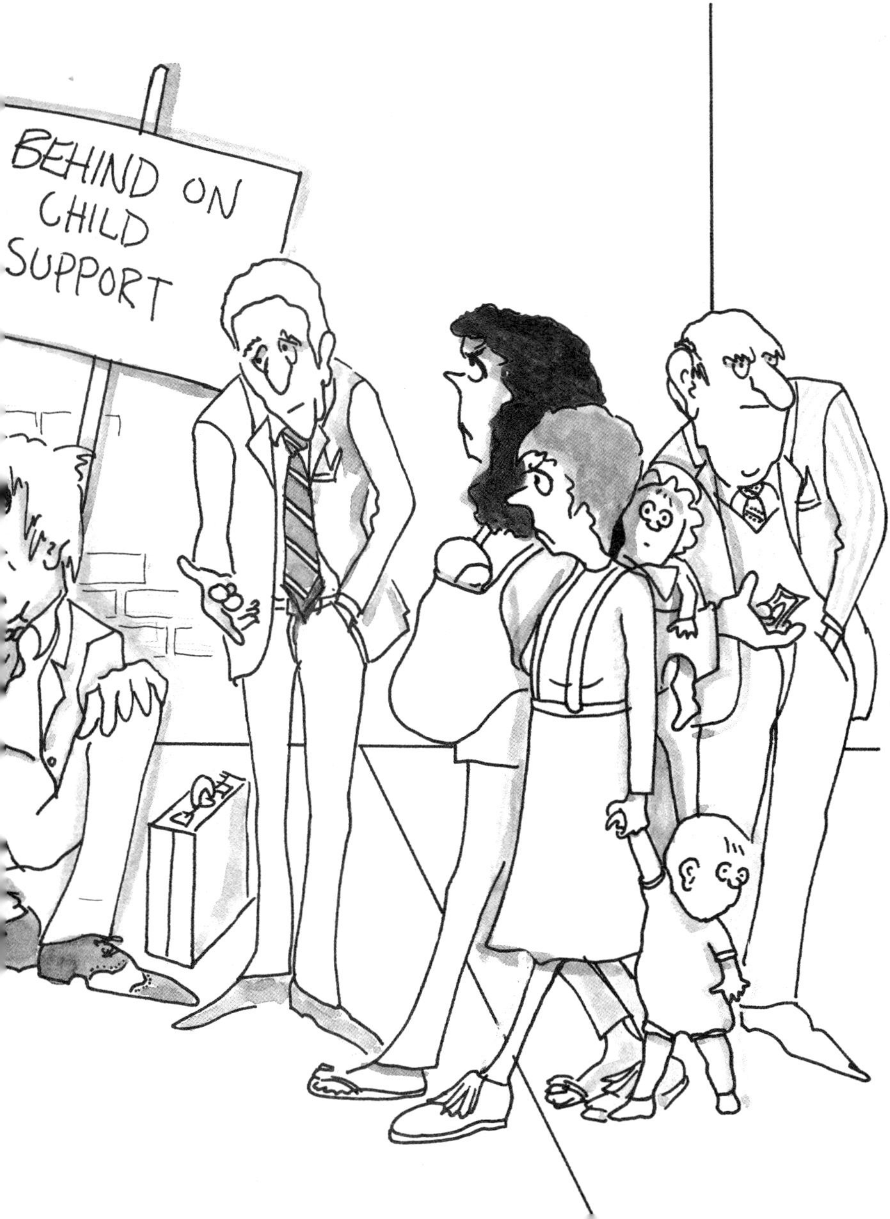
BEHIND ON CHILD SUPPORT

"WAIT JUST A MINUTE WHILE I WRAP A LITTLE PRESENT FOR DADDY!"

MOM ENTERTAINS A
GENTLEMAN IN HER BOUDOIR.

YOU SHOULD READ THIS BOOK, IT'S FULL OF GOOD IDEAS!
HOW TO MEET MEN

TO INCREASE YOUR CHANCES OF MEETING MEN—GET INVOLVED..... VOLUNTEER, TAKE A CLASS.
.... A CLASS? HMMMMmm
HOW TO MEET MEN

LOOK-OUT MEN!! HERE I COME!

SEXY NEW JUMP SUIT!!!!
NEW TOOL BOX......

AUTO MECHANICS
GOOD EVENING LADIES!

WHY CAN'T WE HAVE A VIDEO LIKE LEATHER GODDESSES INSTEAD OF BINGOBUGGLEBEE PRESENTS ?

"DADDY PAYS _FIVE_ DOllARS!"

YOU DON'T HAVE A DAD AT YOUR HOUSE! ....SO, YOU'RE PROB'LY ADOPTED!

?

MOMMY, AM I ADOPTED?
NO!

AM I A ORPHAN?
OF COURSE NOT!

?

O.K., SO WHAT ARE YA CALLED WHEN YA ONLY HAVE A DAD EVERY OTHER WEEKEND?
?

CHRISTM TREES— U—CUT
DADDY'S TREE IS FIREPROOF AND IT GOES UP AND DOWN LIKE AN UMBRELLA!!

THE DREADED PHONE CALL

"YOU TOLD DADDY – NO CANDY!"

I NEED T'GET SOMETHING STRAIGHT! DADDY'S YOUR EX-HUSBAND AND YOU'RE HIS EX-WIFE— ARE WE EX-KIDS?
...DADDY'S MY EX-HUSBAND BECAUSE WE AREN'T MARRIED ANYMORE, BUT HE'S STILL YOUR DADDY AND YOU'RE STILL HIS KIDS, UNDERSTAND?
YEAH!—BUT IS GRIDLOCK HIS EX-DOG?

THE EX
FAMILY
HAROLD AND MAUD'S KIDS
OLIVE'S 2ND
SAM'S 4th
HI!
JOE'S 3RD
HI! PETE'S 1ST
CAROL'S EX
HI! BILL'S MOM
HI! ROGER'S CURRENT
MARY'S 2ND
HI! JOE'S 3RD
AND GEORGE
JOE'S NO TRESPASSING
JOE
JOE IV

ENDED
NION
HI! DAVE 'N DOT
HI! HAROLD AND GRACE'S KIDS
JAN'S EX
BETTY (SLIM'S EX)
HAROLD'S 3RD
HAROLD AND BELLA'S
WALT'S 2ND
BETTY 1ST
DON'T KNOW
JUNE'S PRESENT
JUNE'S FORMER
MIN ROSE WILMA ADA'S EX
RONNIE'S STEP MOTHER
HI! JOYCE AND HAROLD'S

......AND THEY LIVED HAPPILY EVER AFTER!
THE THREE BEARS
-AT LEAST THOSE GUYS ARE NORMAL!! -THERE'S A MOTHER- A FATHER- AN' A BABY AND THEY ALL LIVE IN THE SAME HOUSE!
BEARS ARE NORMAL?
A NORMAL FAMILY HAS A MOTHER AN' A FATHER AN' CHILDREN ALL IN ONE HOUSE!!
-AN' THE MOM STAYS HOME EVERY DAY AN' MAKES DOUBLE-CHOCOLATE FUDGE-BROWNIES FOR THE CHILDREN!
THAT'S NORMAL!
?

...THERE'S USUALLY A DOG OR A CAT OR A GERBIL OR A PARAKEET —MAYBE SOME FISH.... A PET RABBIT?.... — HOW 'BOUT A HORSE FOR THE GIRL???
THE DAD GOES T'WORK TO GET THE MONEY.....
... HEY GRIDLOCK, I THOUGHT OUR FAMILY WAS NORMAL!!
GRIDLOCK

HEY!
PETER RABBIT'S MOM WAS A SINGLE PARENT TOO!
THE TALE OF PETER RABBIT

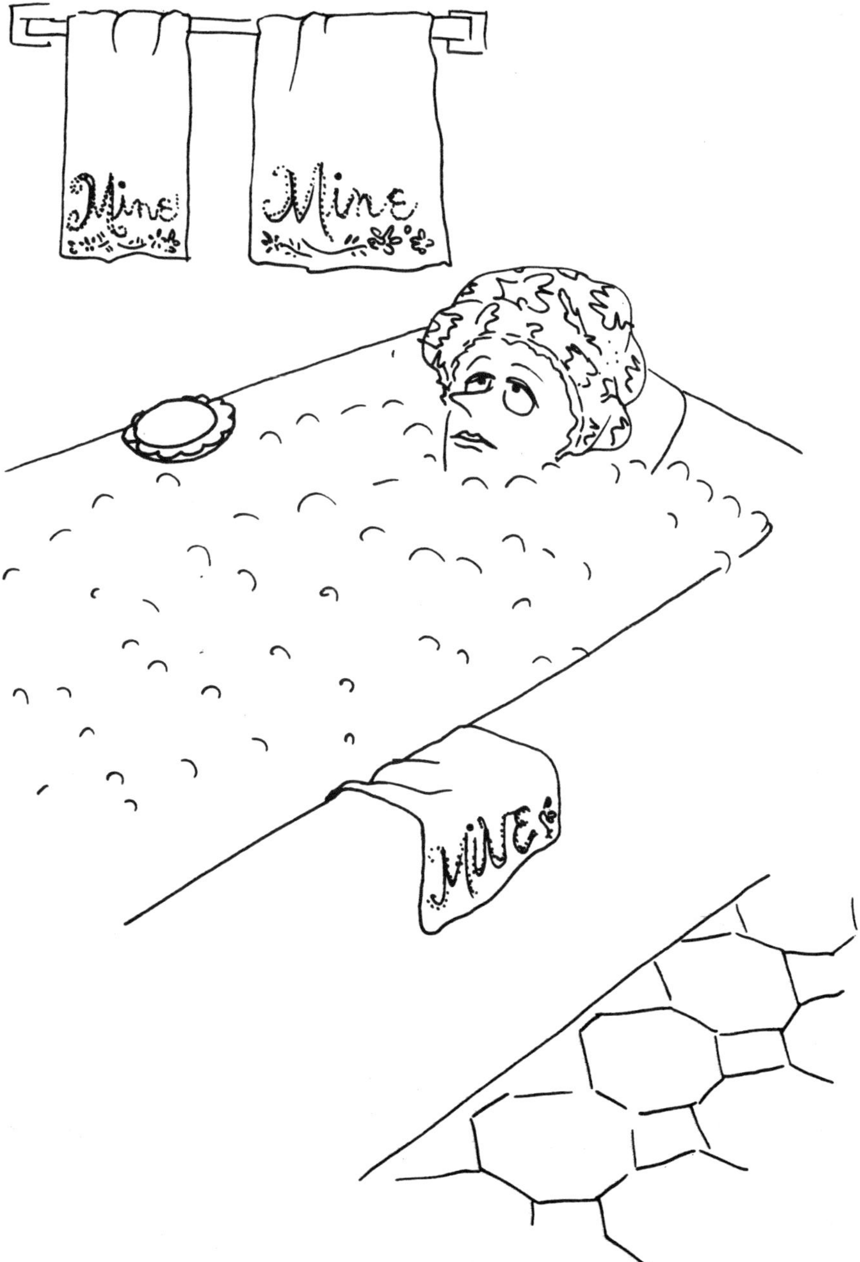
Mine
Mine
MINE